This book belongs to:

Christmas  Connect the Dots Numbers Game Coloring Book

14 15

13 16

12
11 18 17

10 9 20 19

7 22 21
8
6 23

5 4 25 24

26

2
3 28 27
29

1 30

Mary Lou Brown & Sandy Mahony

10

11 •12

•13

9•

8   •14

7•

•15

6•   •16

17

5•
4

18

20

1

19

3

2

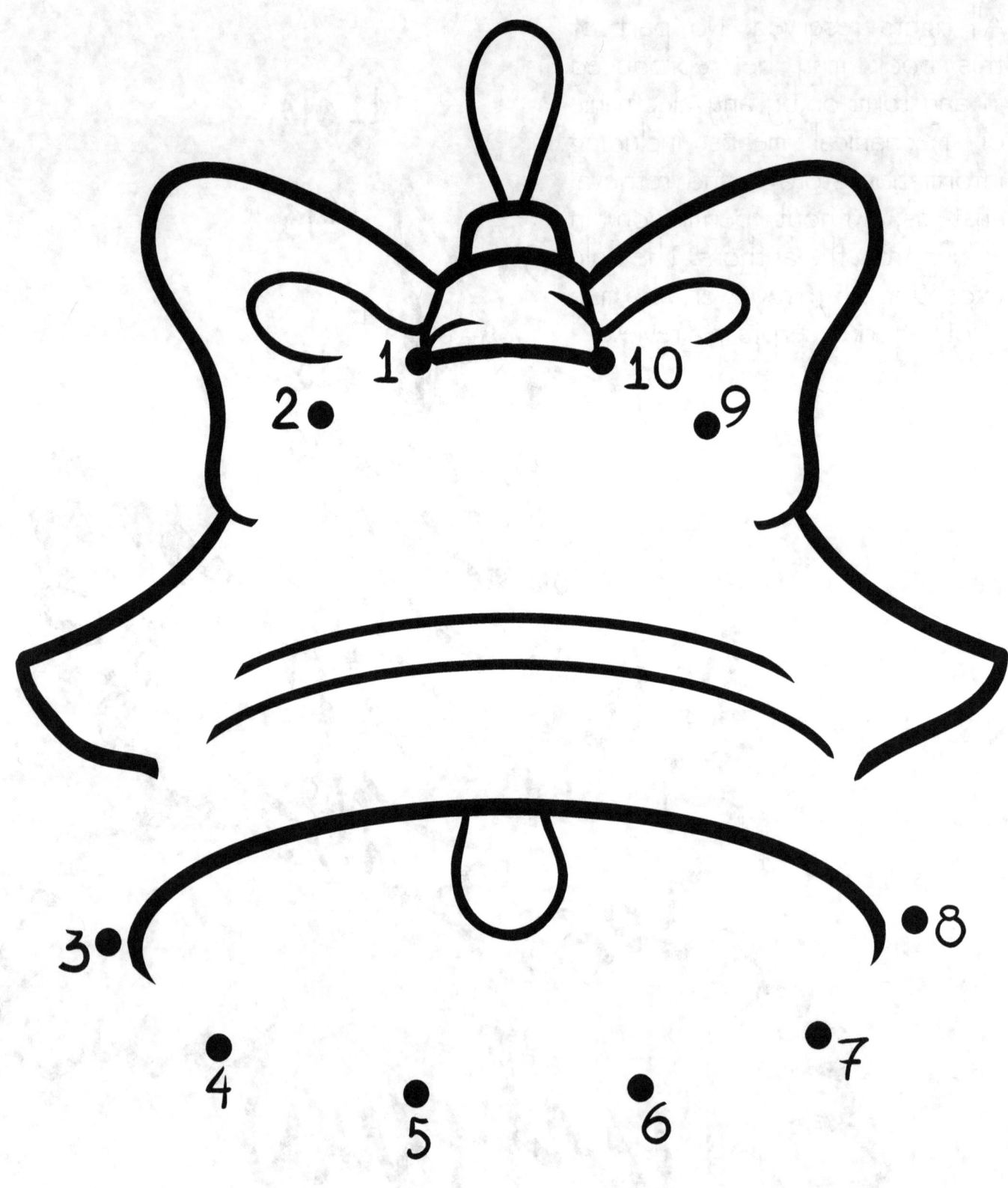

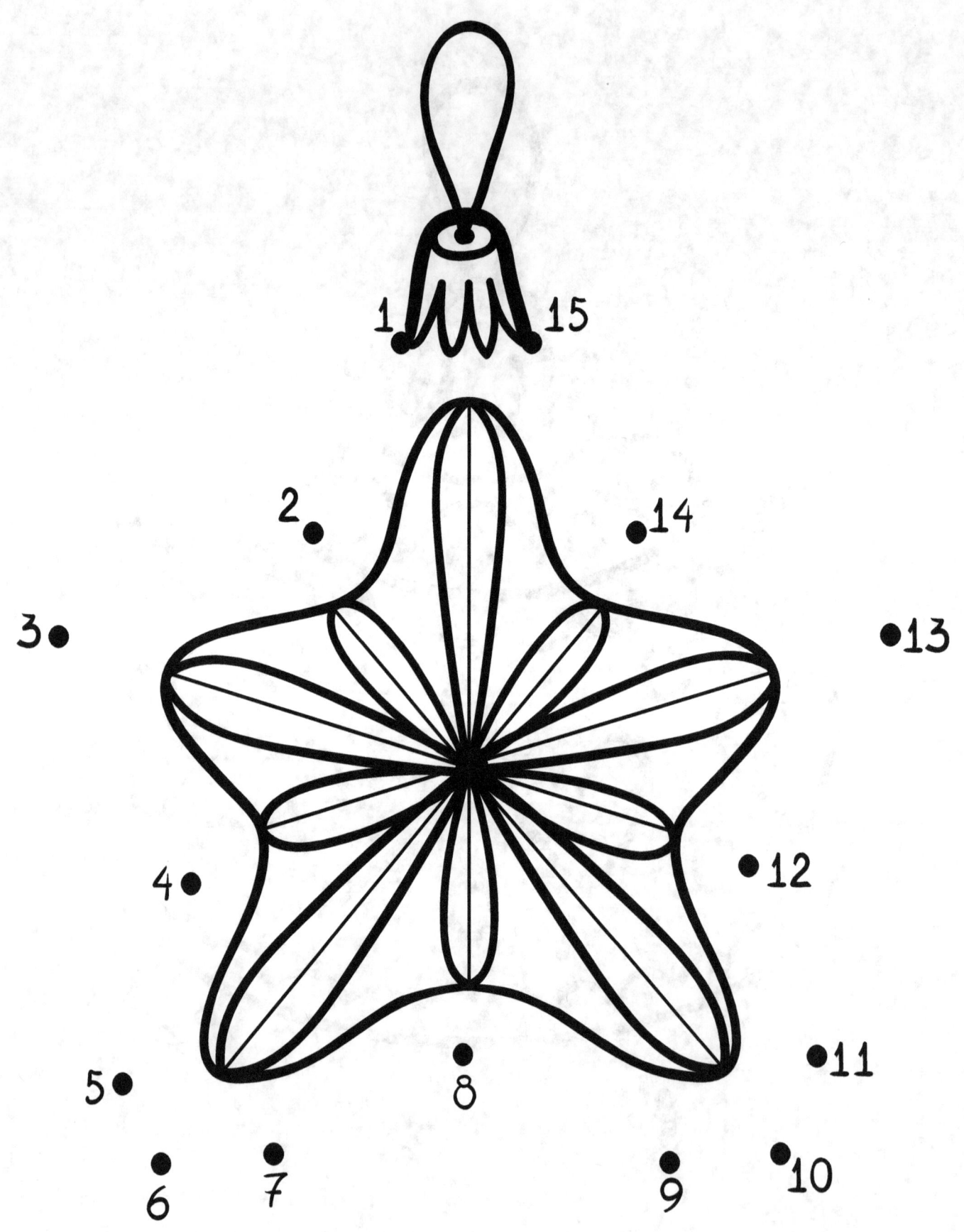

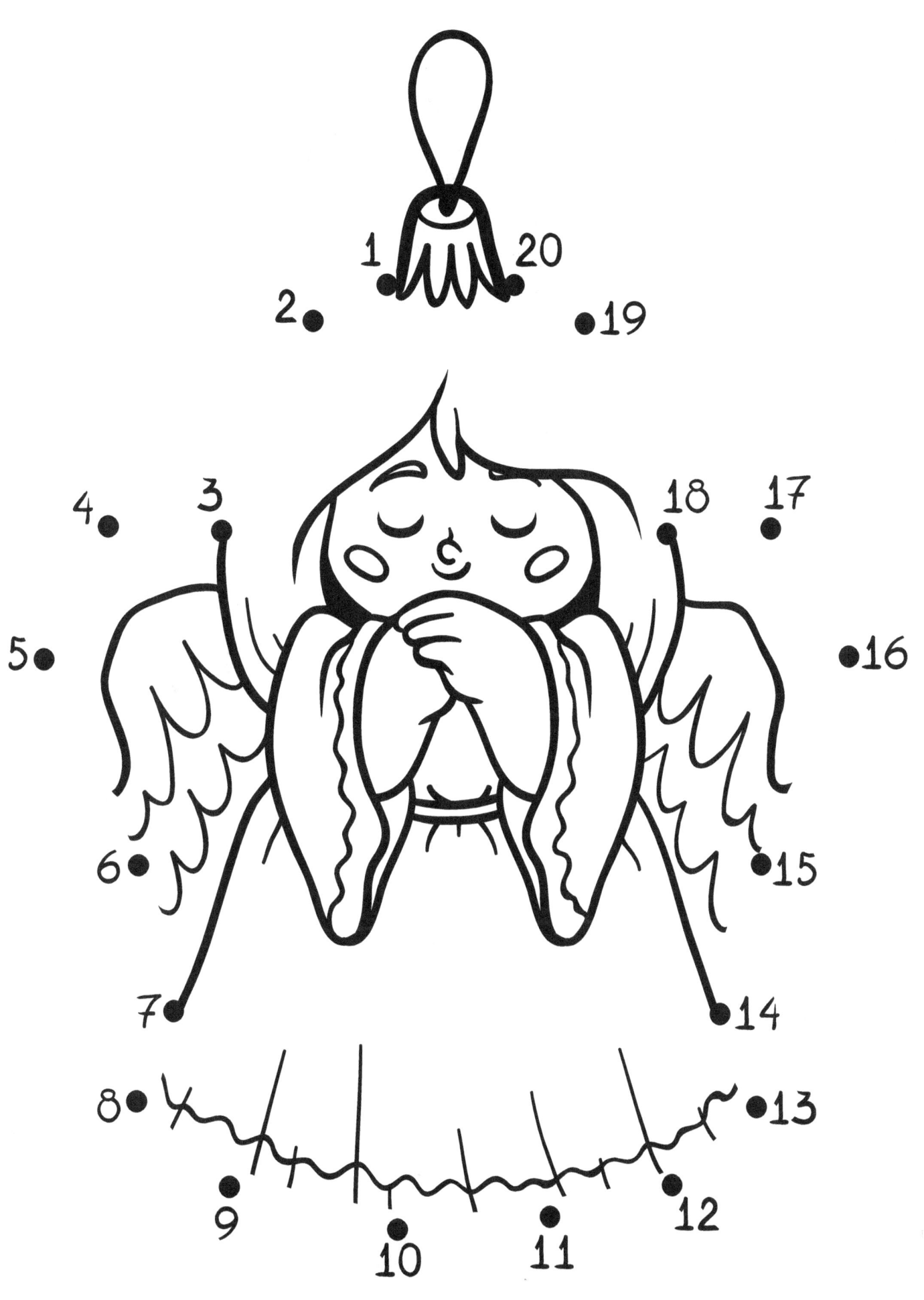

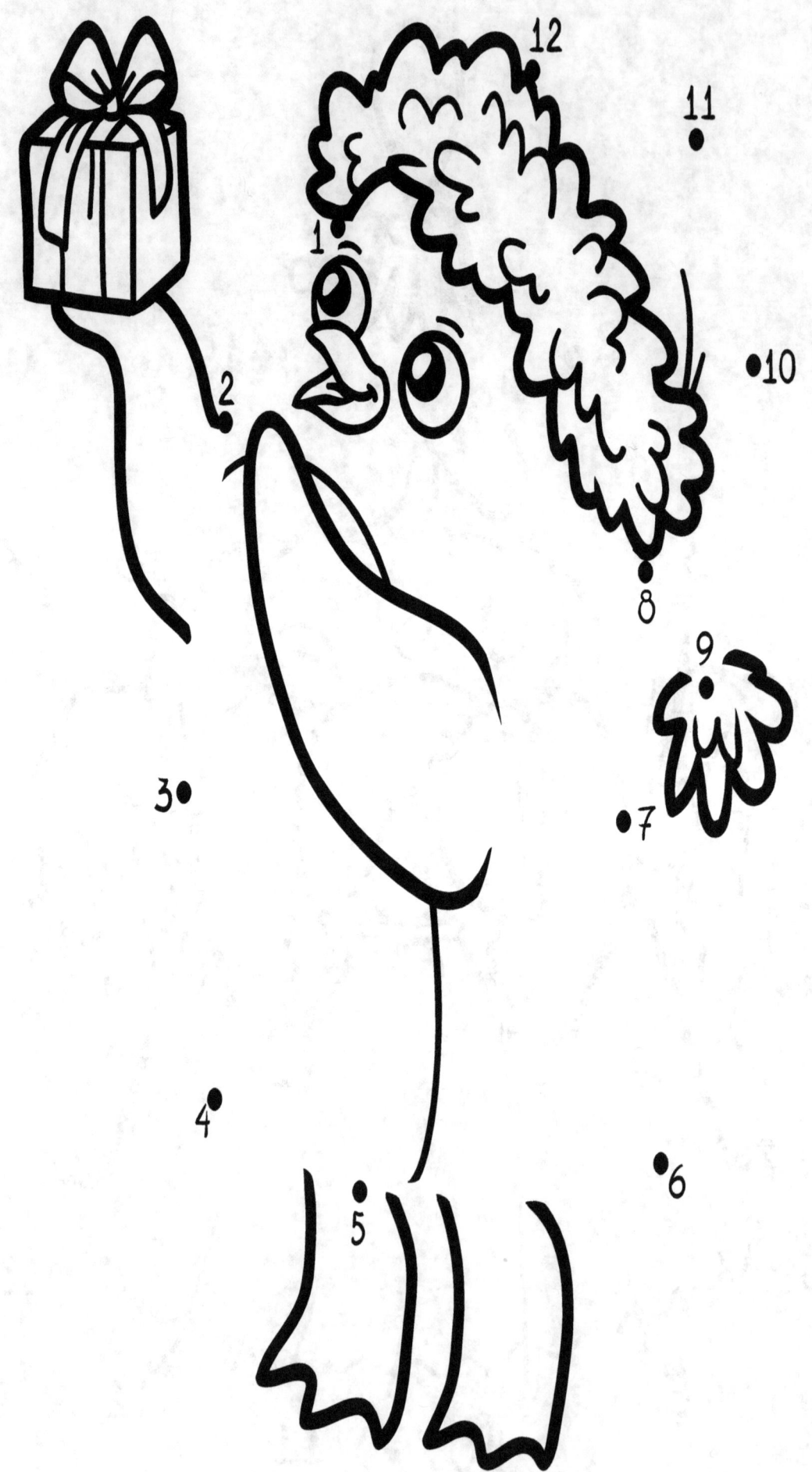

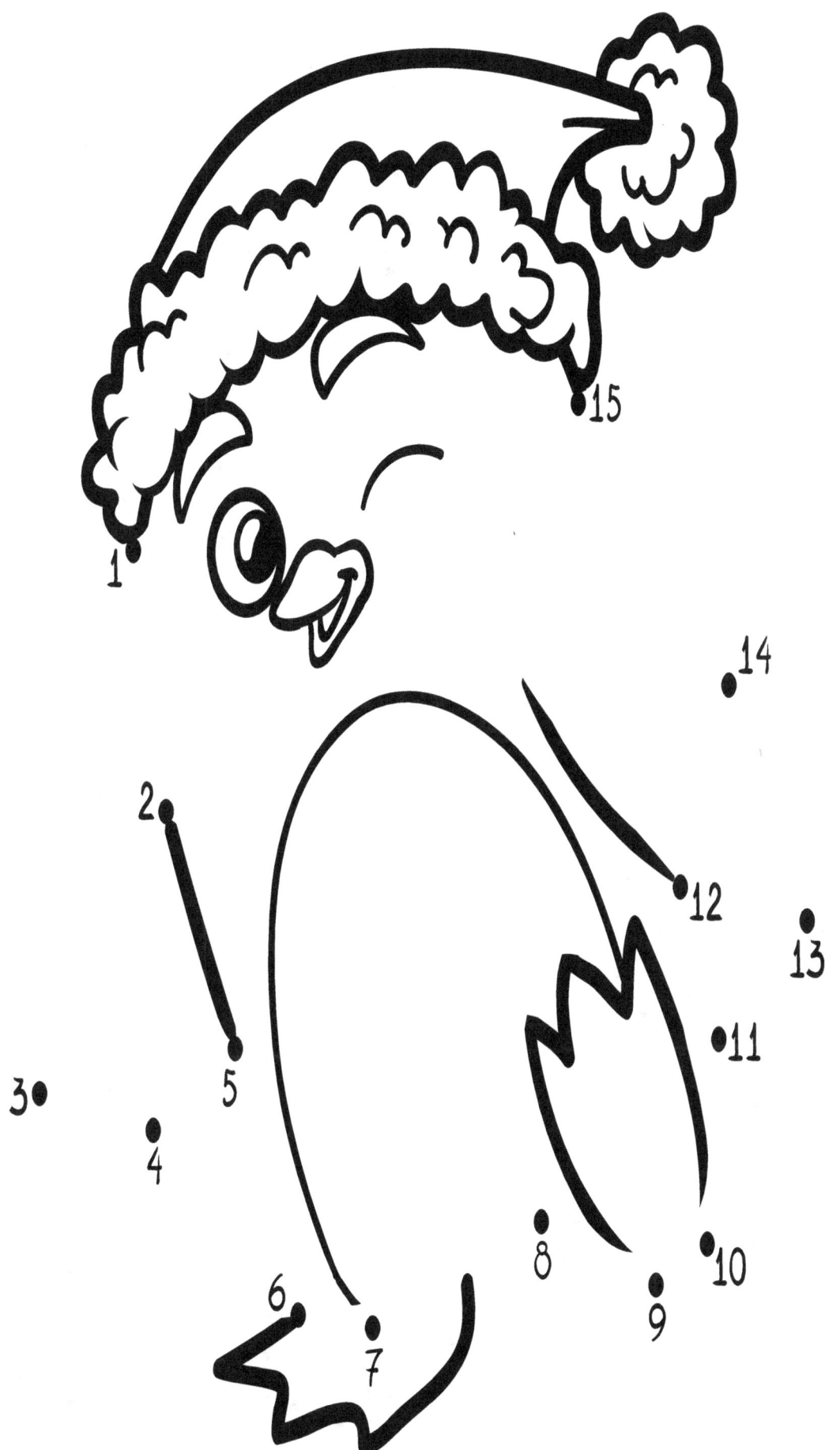

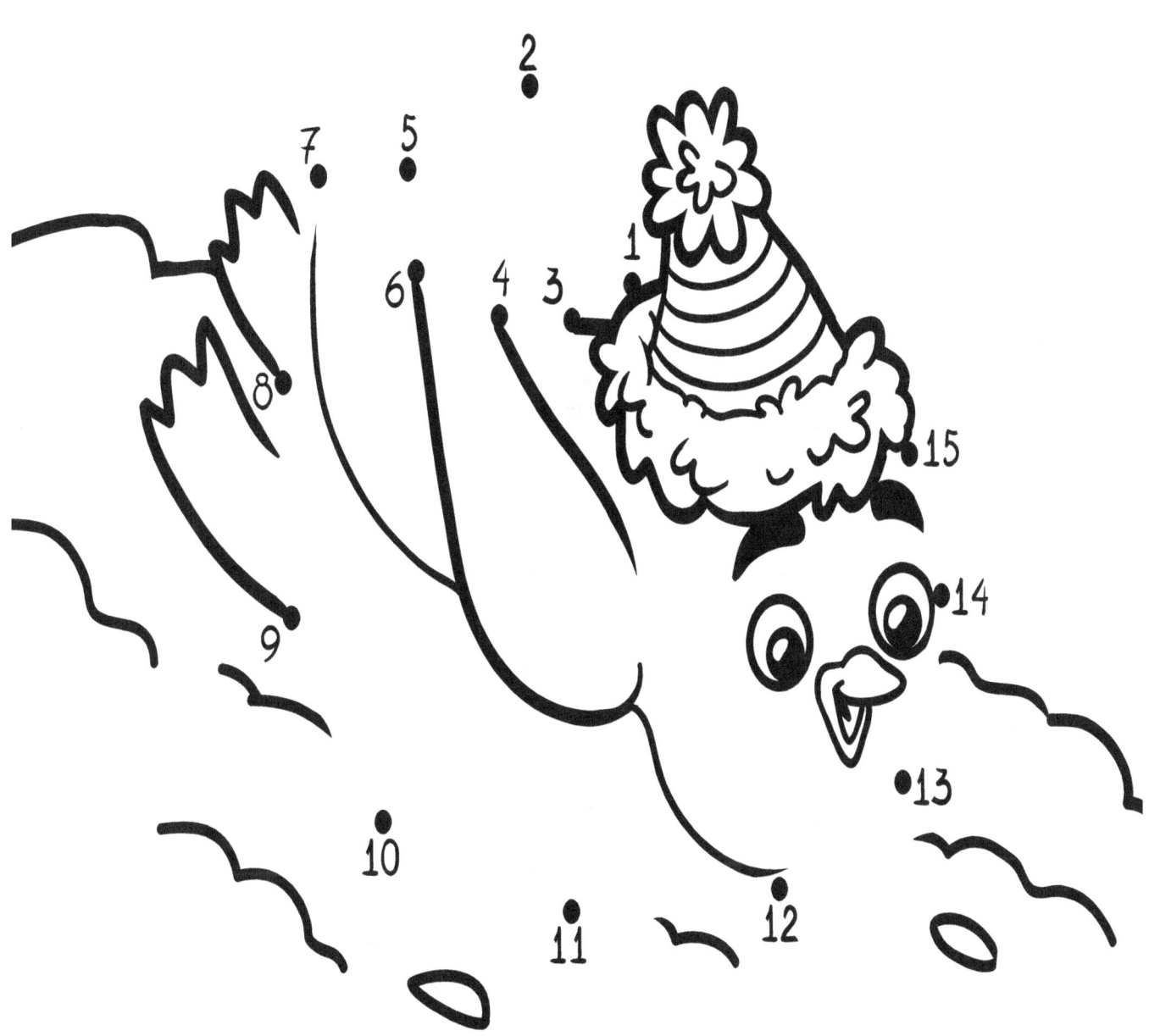

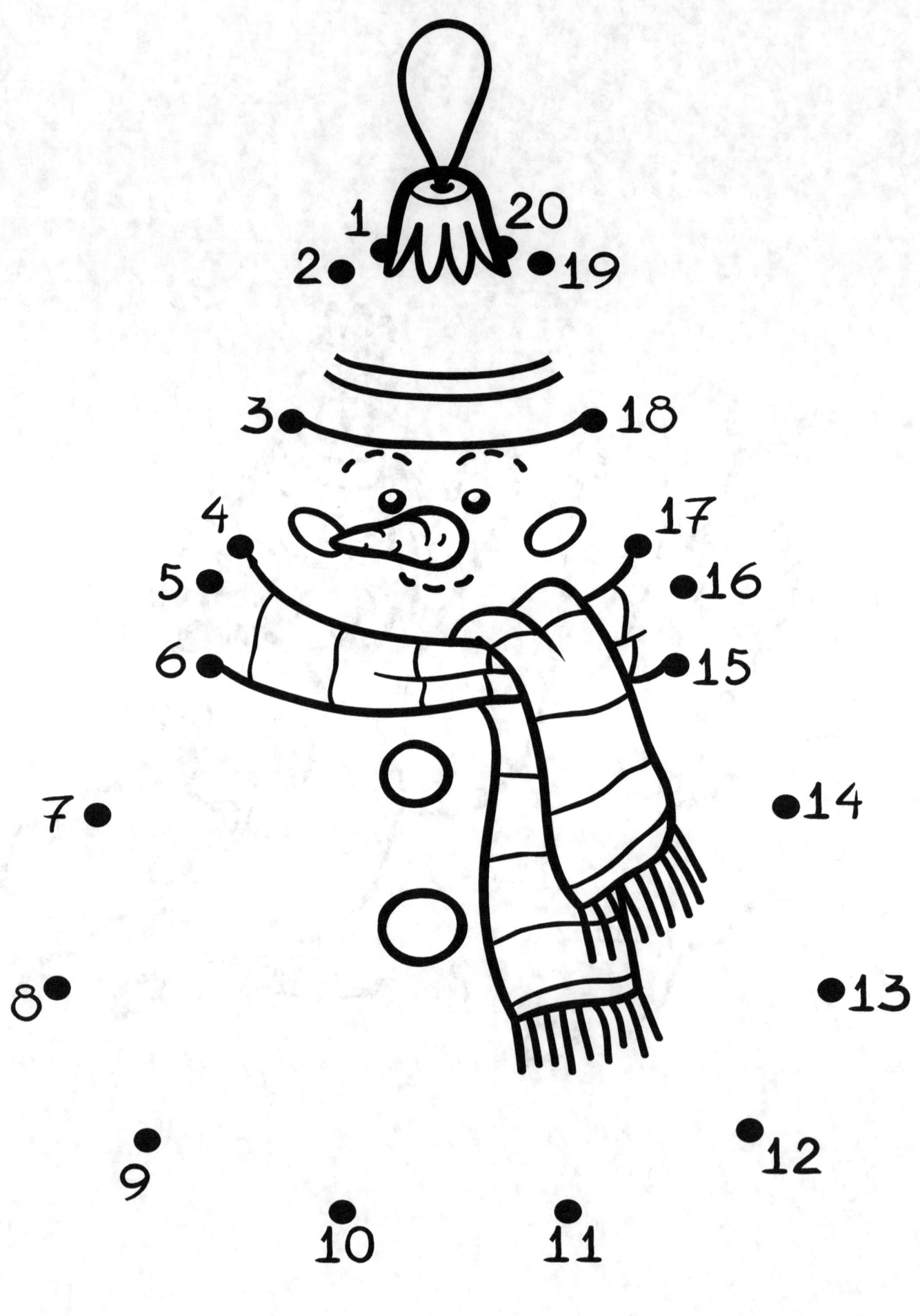

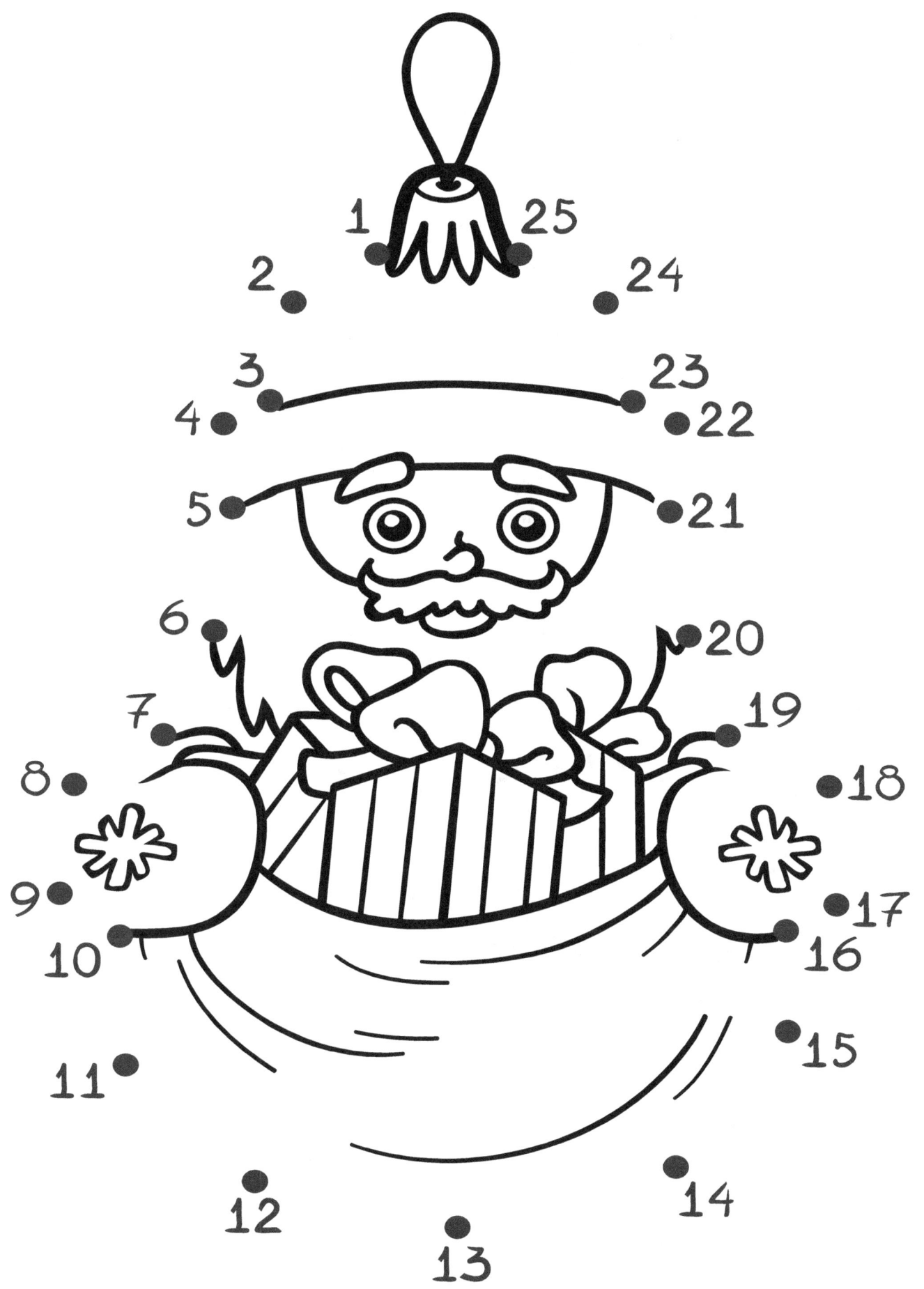

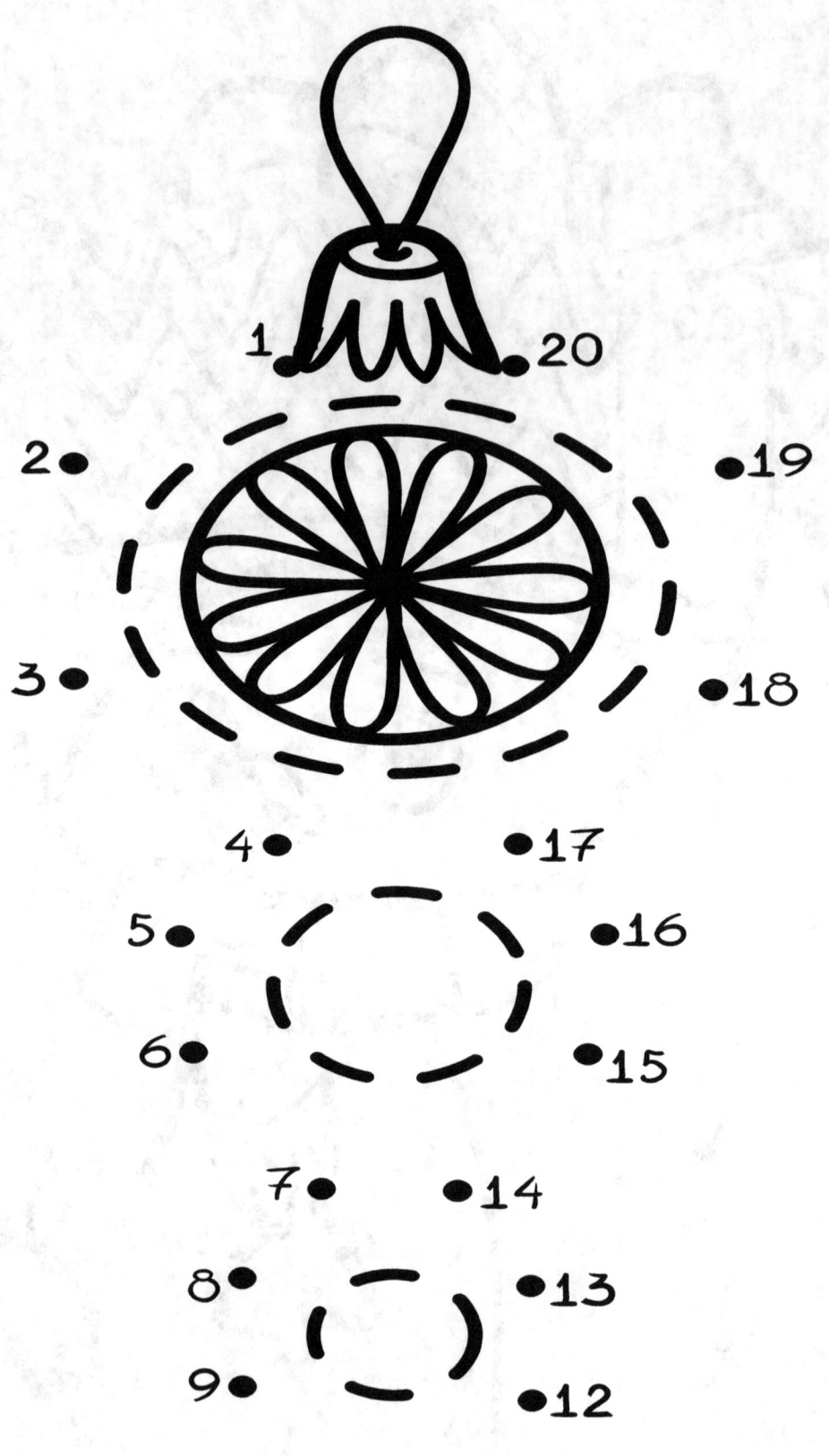

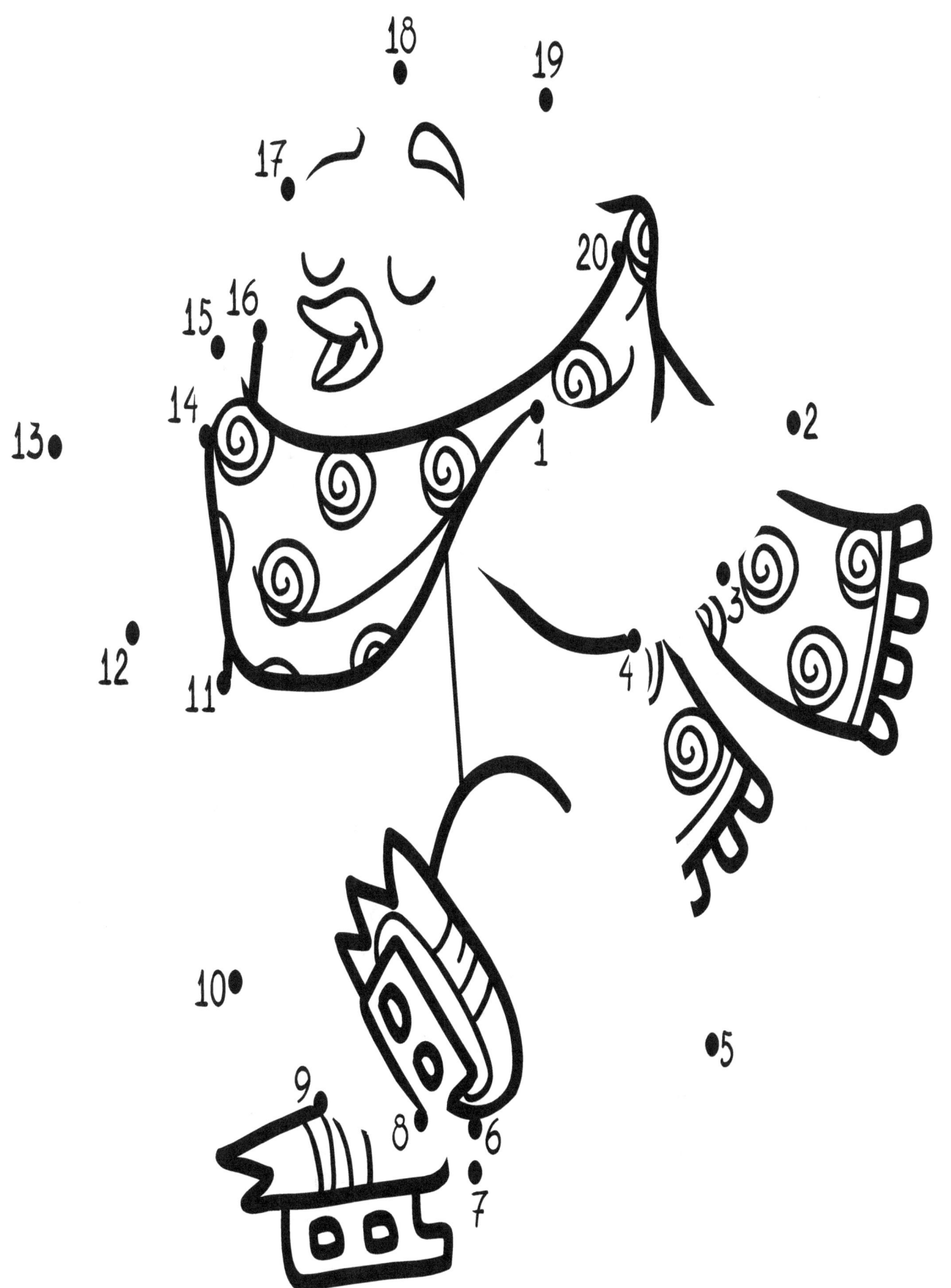

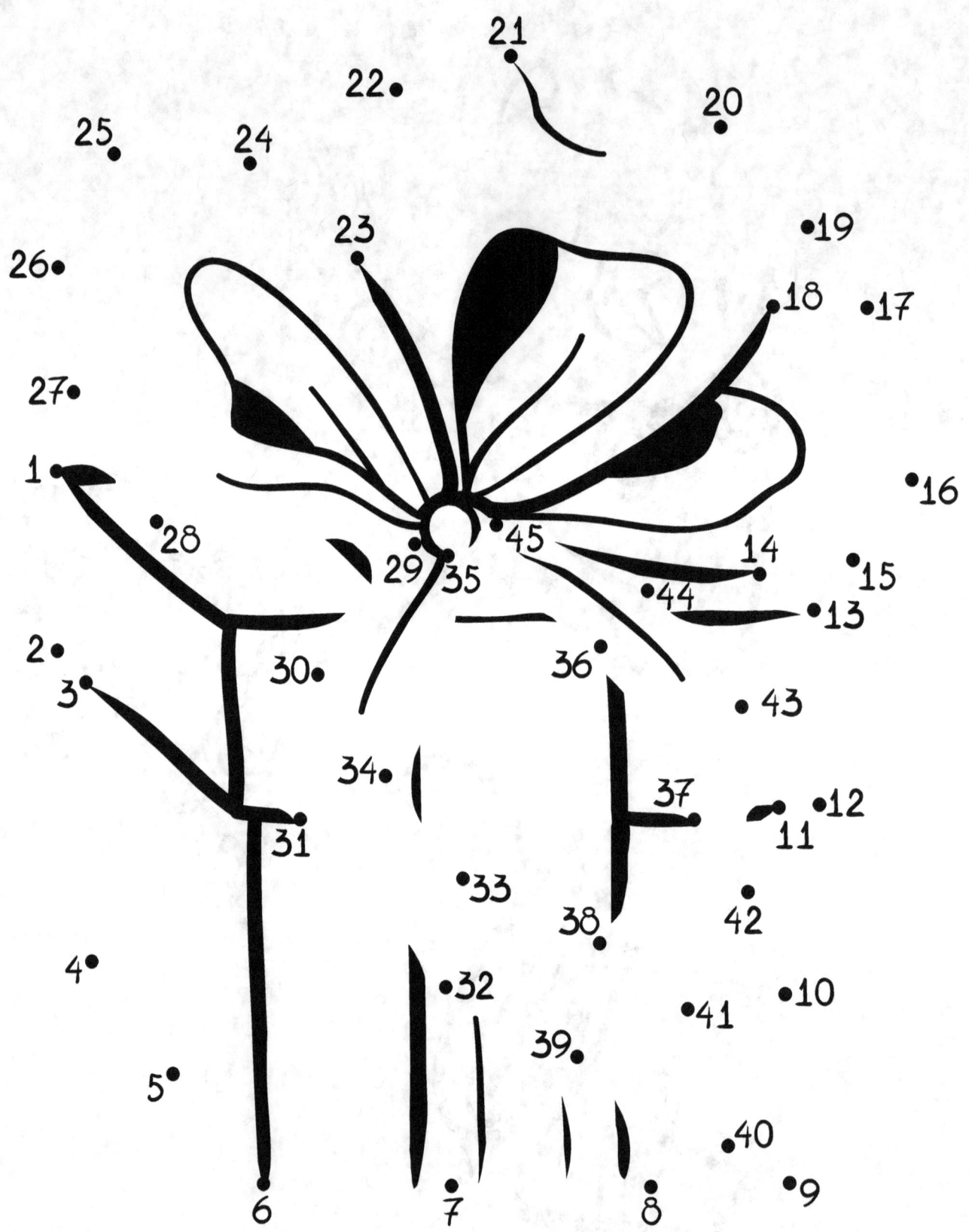

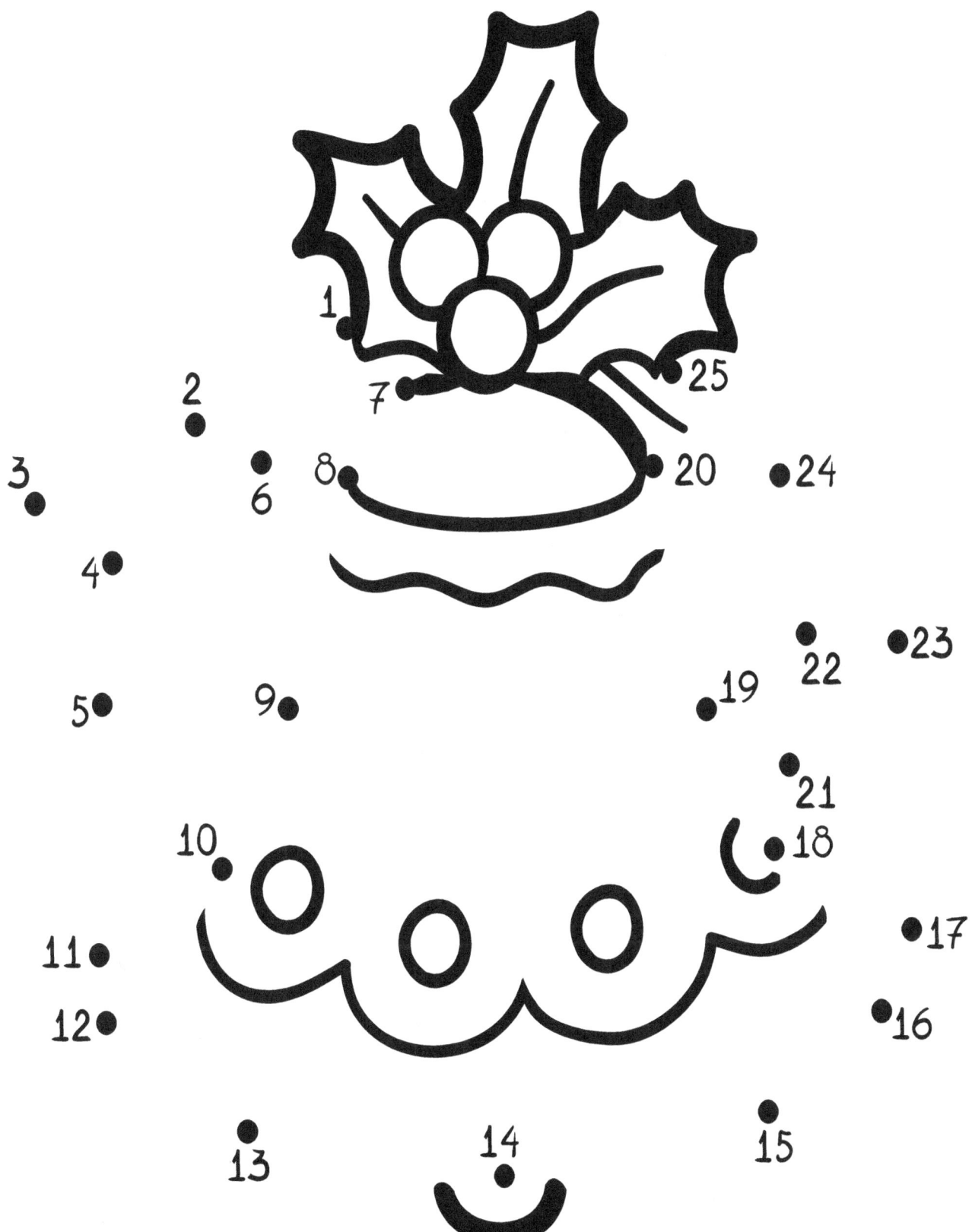

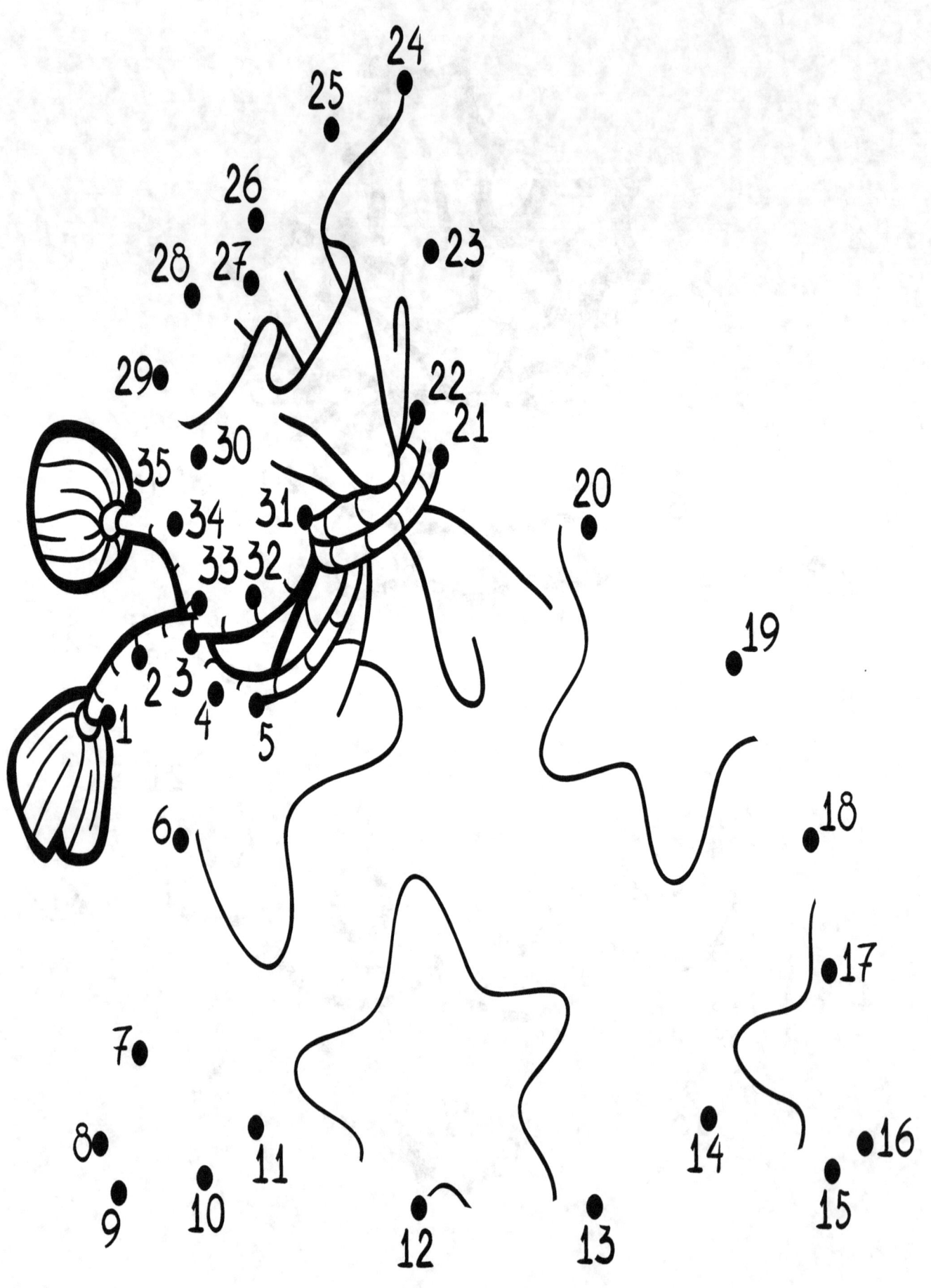

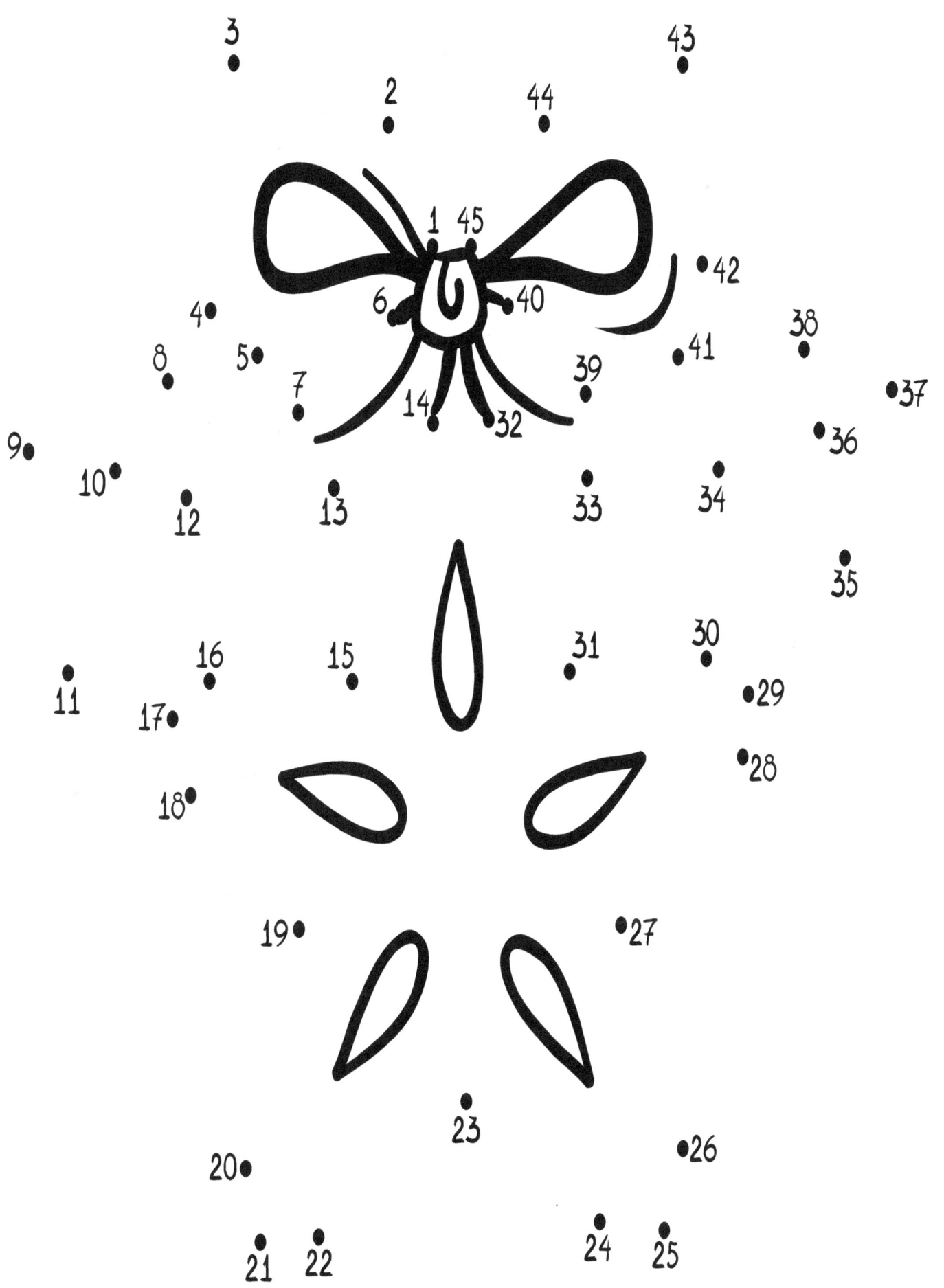

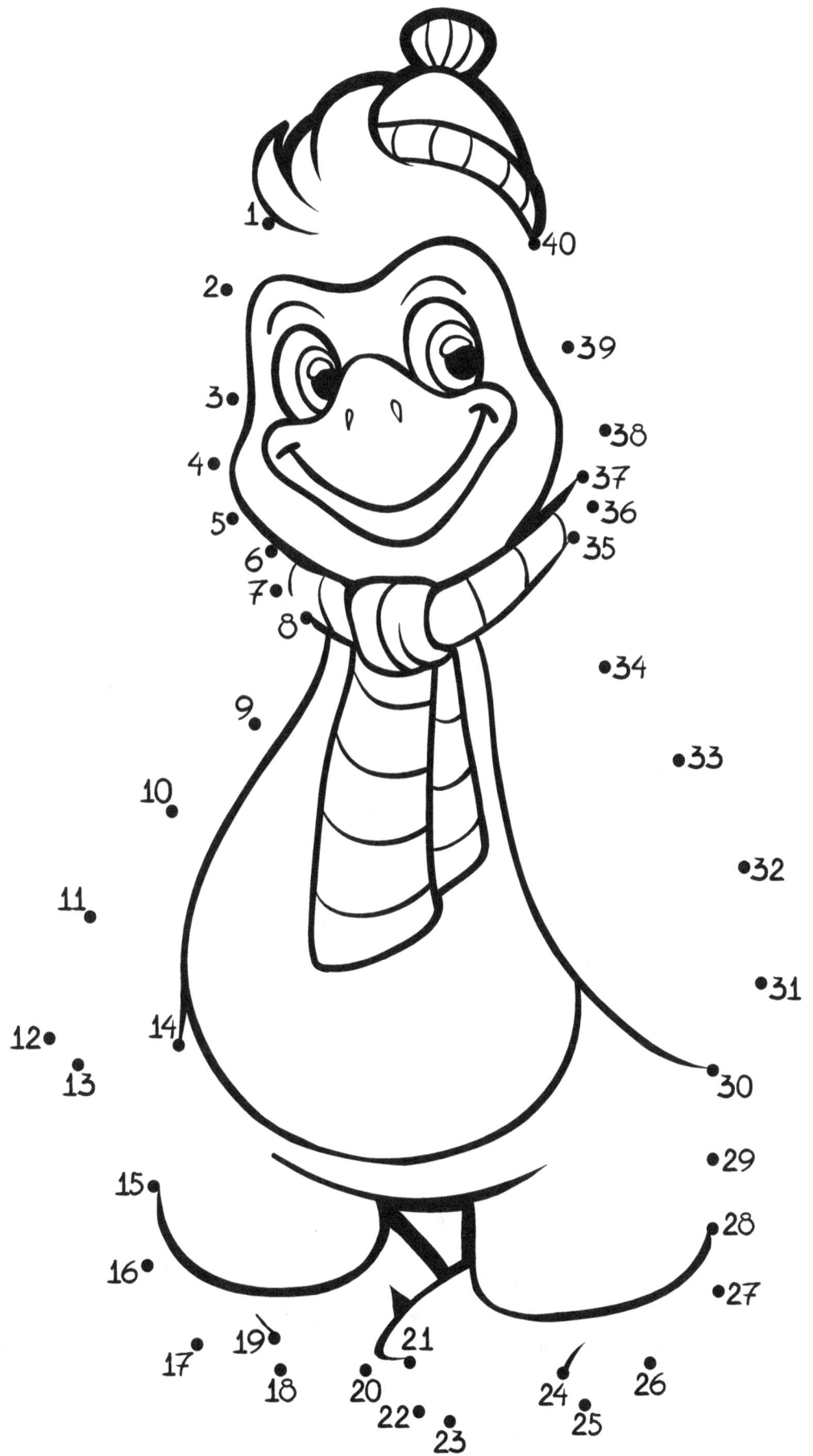

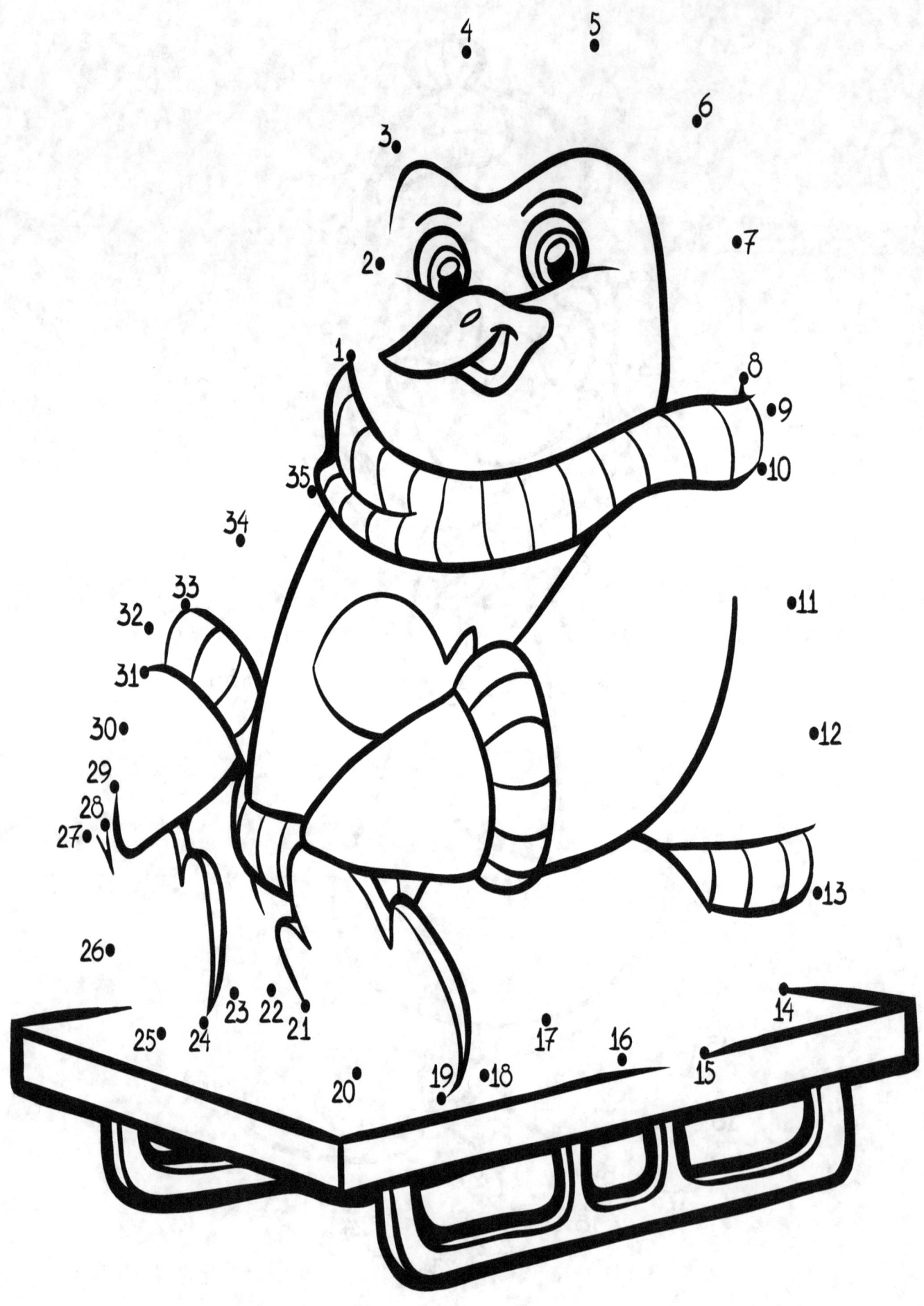

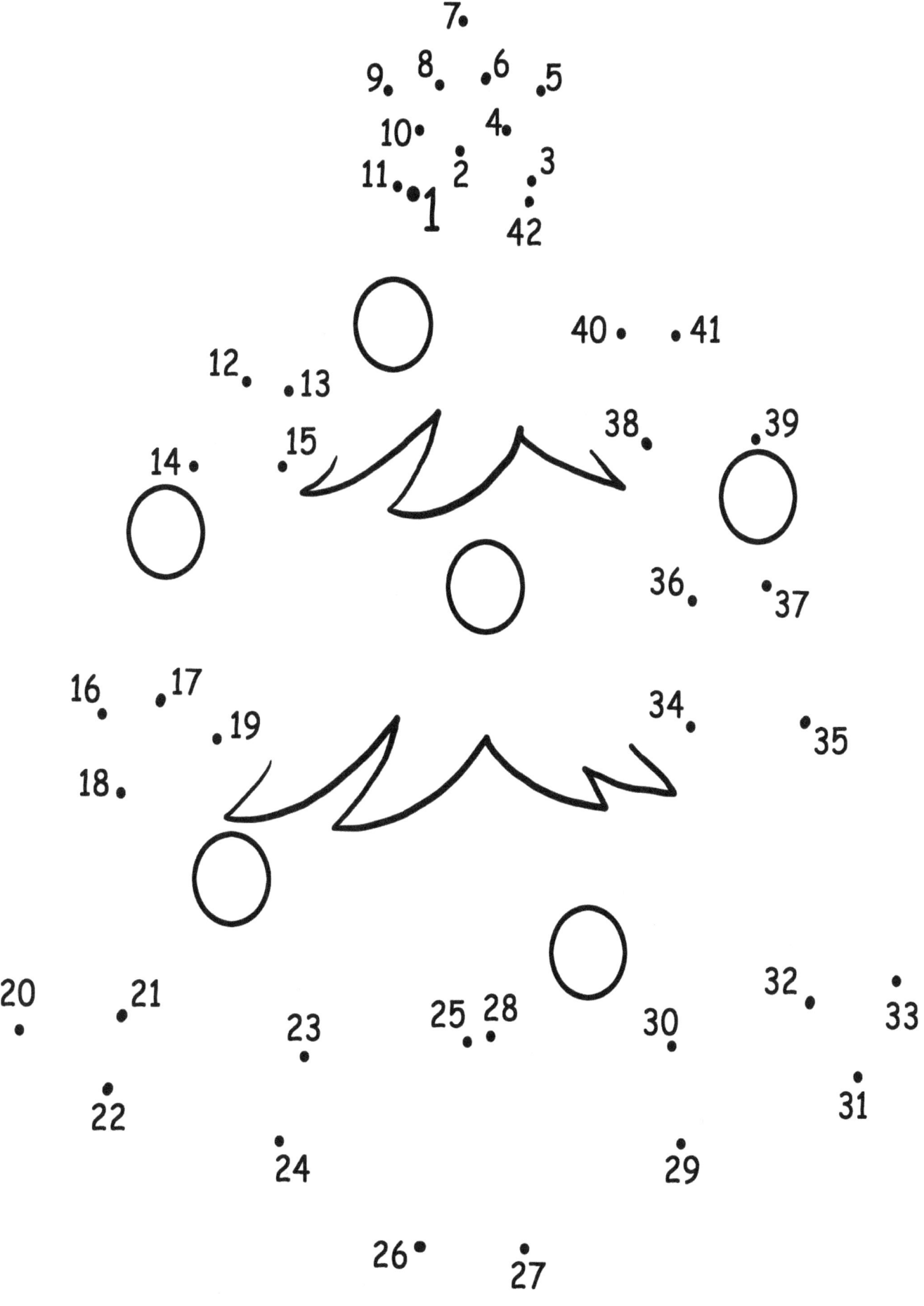

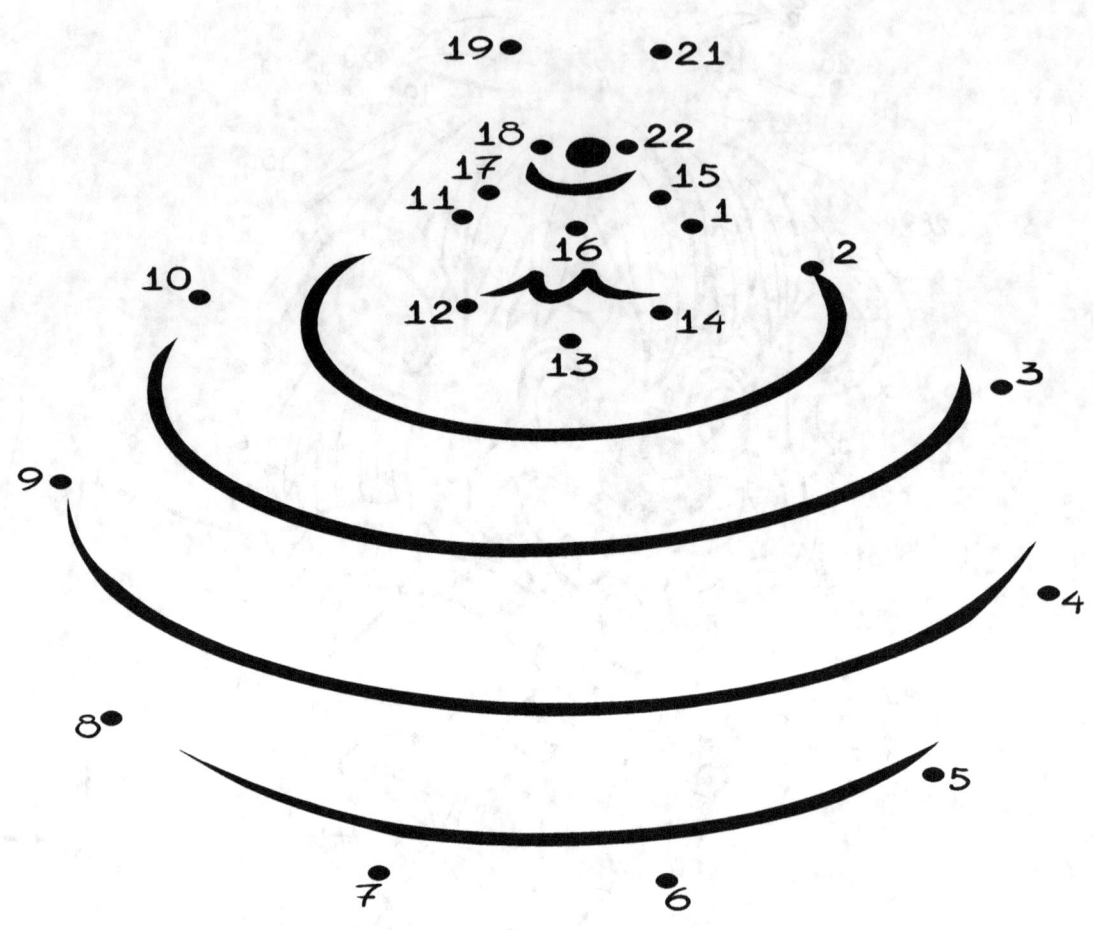

adventurelearningpress.com

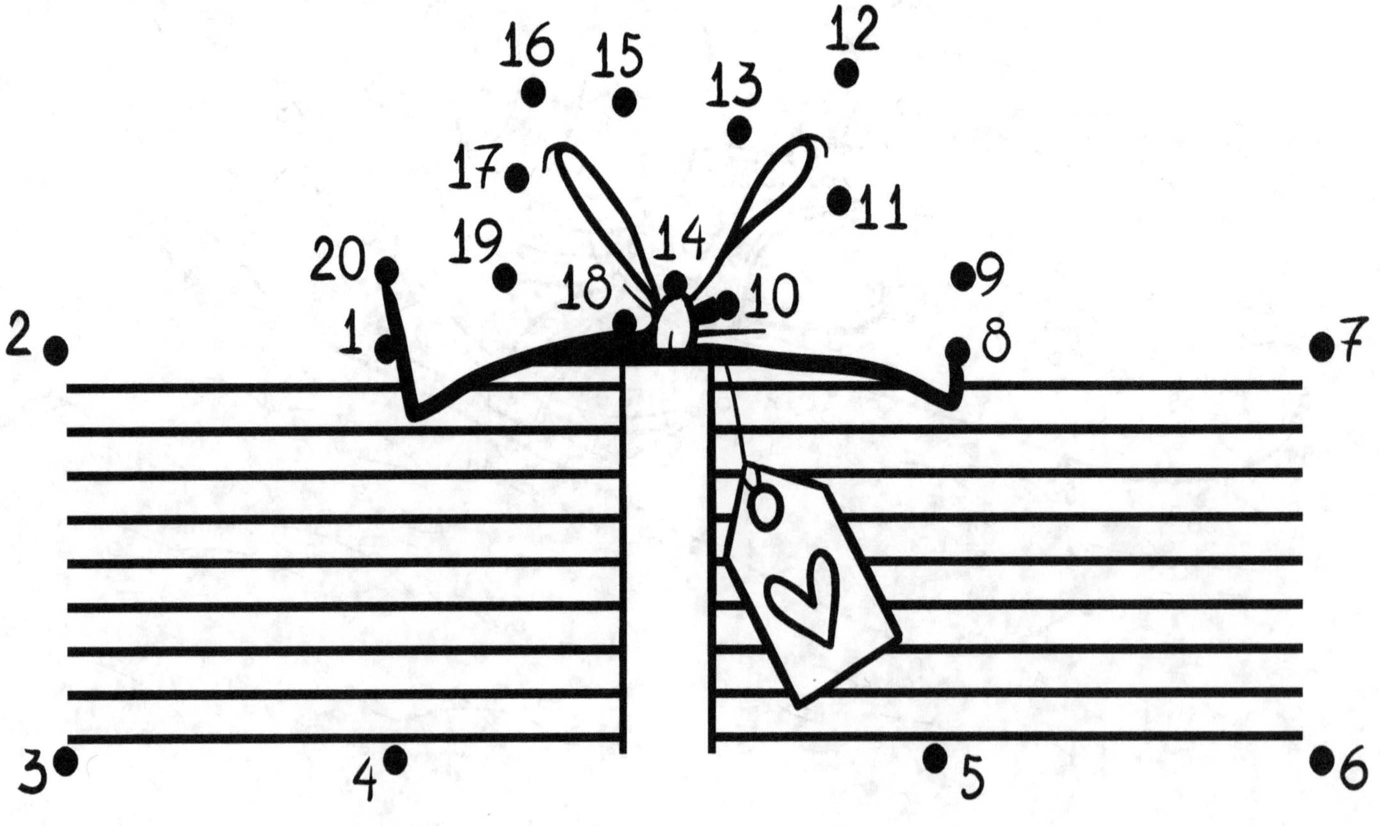

www.ingramcontent.com/pod-product-compliance
Lightning Source LLC
Chambersburg PA
CBHW081804280526
45789CB00008B/2999